Children of the World

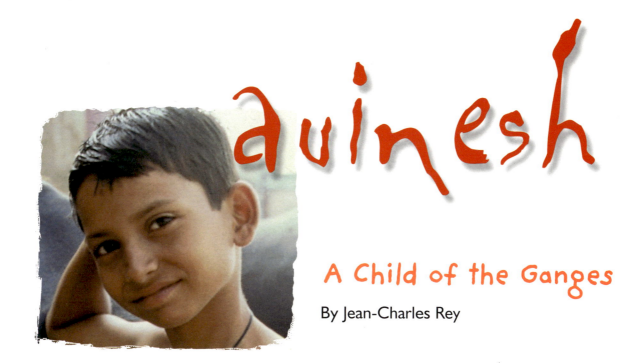

auinesh

A Child of the Ganges

By Jean-Charles Rey

BLACKBIRCH PRESS
An imprint of Thomson Gale, a part of The Thomson Corporation

Detroit • New York • San Francisco • San Diego • New Haven, Conn. • Waterville, Maine • London • Munich

© Éditions PEMF, 2001

First published by PEMF in France as *Avinesh, enfant du Gange*.

First published in North America in 2005 by Thomson Gale.

Thomson and Star Logo are trademarks and Gale and Blackbirch Press are registered trademarks used herein under license.

For more information, contact
Blackbirch Press
27500 Drake Rd.
Farmington Hills, MI 48331-3535
Or you can visit our Internet site at http://www.gale.com

ALL RIGHTS RESERVED.
No part of this work covered by the copyright hereon may be reproduced or used in any form or by any means—graphic, electronic, or mechanical, including photocopying, recording, taping, Web distribution or information storage retrieval systems—without the written permission of the publisher.

Every effort has been made to trace the owners of copyrighted material.

Photo Credits: All photos © Jean-Charles Rey except pages 6, 7, 15, Corel Corporation; Table of Contents collage: EXPLORER/Boutin (upper left); François Goalec (upper middle and right); Muriel Nicolotti (bottom left); CIRIC/Michel Gauvry (bottom middle); CIRIC/Pascal Deloche (bottom right)

LIBRARY OF CONGRESS CATALOGING-IN-PUBLICATION DATA

Rey, Jean-Charles.
   Avinesh : a child of the Ganges / by Jean-Charles Rey.
      p. cm. — (Children of the world)
   ISBN 1-4103-0287-3 (hard cover : alk. paper)
   1. Varanasi (Uttar Pradesh, India)—Juvenile literature. 2. Children—India—Varanasi (Uttar Pradesh)—Juvenile literature. I. Title. II. Series: Children of the world (Blackbirch Press)

DS486.B4R49 2005
954'.2—dc22

2005000696

Printed in the United States of America
10 9 8 7 6 5 4 3 2 1

Contents

Facts About India...5
The State of Uttar Pradesh..6
The Ganges River...7
Benares, a Sacred City...8
Avinesh's Family..10
Bathing the Water Buffaloes.....................................12
Water Buffalo in India..14
Manure: a Precious Commodity....................................16
The Candle Seller...18
Street Performances...20
School..22
Other Books in the Series.......................................24

Facts About India

India is a federal republic made up of 25 states and 7 territories.

Agriculture:	rice, wheat, cotton, tea, sugar cane, cattle raising
Capital:	New Delhi
Government:	parliamentary democracy
Industry:	coal, iron, metals, textiles
Land Area:	1,269,345 square miles (3,290,000 square kilometers)
Languages:	Hindi and English for the Federation and other official languages in each state
Money:	the rupee
Natural Resources:	coal, iron ore, magnesium, mica, bauxite, titanium ore, chromite, natural gas, diamonds, oil, limestone, farmland
Population:	1,065,462,000
Religions:	Hinduism (83%), Islam (12%), Sikhism (2%), Christianity (2%), Buddhism (1%)

The State of Uttar Pradesh

Uttar Pradesh is the most populated state in India and one of the most industrialized. It is located in the plain of the Ganges River.

The Ganges River

The source of the Ganges is in the Himalayas, at nearly 14,763 feet (4,500 meters). The river flows 1,292 miles (2,080 kilometers) through India.

The Ganges River is an important part of life in India.

Benares, a Sacred City

The city of Benares is in the Indian state of Uttar Pradesh. It was built alongside the Ganges. This large city of more than 1 million inhabitants is sacred to both Hindus and Buddhists.

Many Hindu pilgrims come to Benares to do their ablutions. They purify their bodies in the sacred water of the Ganges.

Many come also to scatter the ashes of the dead in the sacred river. They do this after the bodies have been burned.

Indians believe that this helps the soul of the dead person be reincarnated, or reborn, in another body.

Above: The roofs of the old part of Benares.

Left: The banks of the Ganges at dawn. People wash both their bodies and their clothes in the river.

Below: The poor neighborhoods are overpopulated and badly maintained.

Avinesh's Family

Avinesh lives with his family in a poor neighborhood of Benares. He has many brothers and sisters. His parents own a farm where the children also work.

Avinesh is nine years old. He wears a pendant around his neck. It represents a divinity.

The grandmother takes care of the house. She wears a sari, the traditional dress of Indian women.

Mitra, seven years old, is one of Avinesh's sisters.

Avinesh's family owns a few cows. They drink the cows' milk or sell it. However, the cows are not killed for their meat, because they are sacred to the Hindus.

Rice, tomatoes, and chickpeas are rolled up in a kind of pancake called a chapati. Indian food is very spicy.

Milking the cows at the family's farm. The manure collects in the middle of the courtyard.

Bathing the Water Buffaloes

Every morning, Avinesh takes charge of the water buffaloes in his neighborhood. Each owner gives him a few rupees for washing his buffalo.

Armed with his stick, Avinesh guides them to the Ganges.

The bridge marks the limit of Benares. This is where the buffaloes bathe, as well as the "untouchables," the lowest caste, or class, of society.

Buffaloes like water. Every day, the water buffalo need to be bathed. Parasites are removed from their ears and horns.

The majority of the herd is made up of females. There are only one or two males.

Avinesh's older brother accompanies him. He helps control the males.

Taking care of water buffalo is boys' work.

Above: During their bath, Avinesh jumps from buffalo to buffalo to get rid of the parasites on each animal.

Left: Avinesh gets out of the Ganges while his older brother takes care of the last buffaloes.

Water Buffalo in India

Water buffalo are valuable in India. People drink their milk, eat their meat,

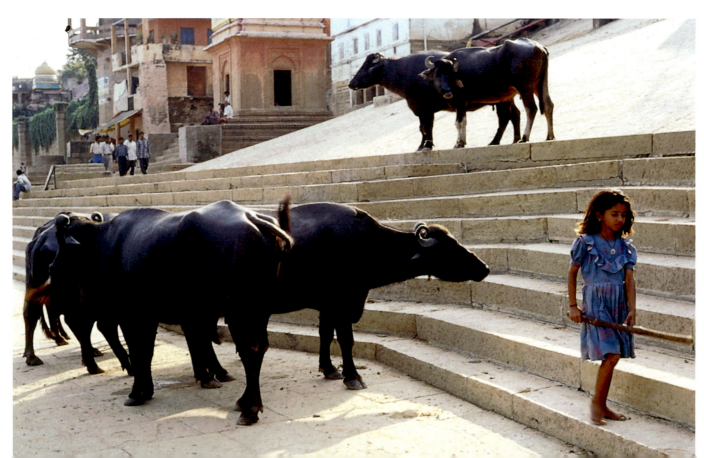

Collecting cow and water buffalo manure is an important daily chore.

and use their manure, or droppings. Cow and buffalo manure is carefully collected on farms and in the streets.

Manure: a Precious Commodity

Girls transport the manure in baskets, which they empty at the bottom of a wall of their house. Then, with their hands, they make cakes and stick them on the wall.

Once the cakes are dry, they are peeled off and sold as fuel. This method is used throughout India.

Wood is rare and used only for burning dead bodies at funerals. Benares is the city of cremations.

Above: Using the walls of a house is very smart when one has little space.

Left: This young girl dries manure cakes on the bank of the Ganges before she sells them.

The Candle Seller

Kerane, who is seven years old, has no brothers. Girls are considered less important than boys in India. They say, "To bring up a girl is to grow a flower in my neighbor's garden." This is because once a girl marries, she moves in with her husband to take care of his parents.

Above: Kerane sells her candles for two rupees apiece.

Left: Kerane with her sisters and her mother (in red).

Left: In the morning, you can see little multicolored floats made of a leaf, flowers, and a candle drifting on the Ganges.

Below: Getting washed. Life is difficult, but joy is present.

Kerane and her sisters must make and sell candles to earn a living. Religion is a big part of the daily life of Indians. During the morning prayer, they set candles afloat on the Ganges. This is an offering to the gods. Kerane sells her colored candles from a woven basket to Hindu pilgrims.

Street Performances

Boys and girls perform on the streets of Benares. These performers are called buskers. The children earn some money from the spectators. However, this is not allowed by the police, who chase the performers away.

Inset: A street performance.

Right: A balancing act with found materials.

Above: As unbelievable as it seems, this little girl is able to lift the heavy rock by the cord around her neck.

Right: The color blue and the fake snake around this boy's neck represent the god Shiva, one of the main deities of Hinduism.

The children amaze bystanders with their flexibility and strength. Some of them are made up to look like religious figures.

School

In Benares, only half the children go to school. The others are too poor to study. They have to work and earn money.

On the way to school, children carry book bags on their backs.

Above: Some children go to school in a rickshaw, a kind of taxi pulled by a man on foot or on a bike.

Students have to buy a uniform and supplies.

The youngest children study in the covered courtyard.

Girls and boys are together in the same class, but girls go to school much less frequently than boys. Class is taught in the official language of the particular state, as well as in English. Hindi is the official language in Uttar Pradesh.

Other Books in the

Arafat: A Child of Tunisia
Asha: A Child of the Himalayas
Ballel: A Child of Senegal
Basha: A Hmong Child
Frederico: A Child of Brazil
Ituko: An Inuit Child

Kradji: A Child of Cambodia
Kuntai: A Masai Child
Leila: A Tuareg Child
Madhi: A Child of Egypt
Thanassis: A Child of Greece
Tomasino: A Child of Peru

16.32